CITY MACHINES

GARBAGE TRUCKS

Connor Dayton

PowerKiDS press

New York

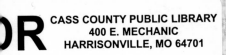

Published in 2012 by The Rosen Publishing Group, Inc.
29 East 21st Street, New York, NY 10010

First Edition

Editor: Jennifer Way
Book Design: Ashley Drago

Photo Credits: Cover, pp. 6, 9, 13, 24 (top left) © www.iStockphoto.com/Mike Clarke; pp. 4–5, 22, 24 (bottom left) Shutterstock.com; pp. 10, 18 Don Mason/Getty Images; pp. 14, 24 (bottom right) © www.iStockphoto.com/Sava Miokovic; p. 17 © www.iStockphoto.com/dlHunter; pp. 21, 24 (top right) Comstock/Thinkstock.

Library of Congress Cataloging-in-Publication Data

Dayton, Connor.
 Garbage trucks / by Connor Dayton. — 1st ed.
     p. cm. — (City machines)
 Includes index.
 ISBN 978-1-4488-4958-1 (library binding) — ISBN 978-1-4488-5066-2 (pbk.) — ISBN 978-1-4488-5067-9 (6-pack)
 1. Refuse and refuse disposal—Juvenile literature. 2. Refuse collection vehicles—Juvenile literature. I. Title.
 TD792.D395 2012
 628.4'42—dc22
                        2010048675

Manufactured in the United States of America

CPSIA Compliance Information: Batch #WS11PK: For Further Information contact Rosen Publishing, New York, New York at 1-800-237-9932

CONTENTS

Garbage trucks pick up trash. They also take trash to a **landfill**.

Most city garbage trucks are **rear loaders**. The trash goes into the back.

Garbage trucks have **compactors**. They squeeze the trash.

The compactor is loud! People wear special earmuffs when working near it.

A crew of people picks up garbage. Paper goods are the most common things in trash.

Some garbage trucks also pick up **recycling**.

Side-loading garbage trucks have arms. Arms do the work of a crew.

Side-loading trucks have one-person crews. The driver controls everything.

Garbage trucks take trash to a landfill. There the trash is buried.

The emptied garbage truck goes back to work!

WORDS TO KNOW

compactor

landfill

rear loader

recycling

INDEX

WEB SITES

Due to the changing nature of Internet links, PowerKids Press has developed an online list of Web sites related to the subject of this book. This site is updated regularly. Please use this link to access the list:
www.powerkidslinks.com/city/garbage/